Dedicated to the memory of Dudley Iles,
a wonderful man and environmentalist whose garden was the inspiration for this story

Crumps Barn Studio
Syde, Cheltenham GL53 9PN
www.crumpsbarnstudio.co.uk

Text © Dinah Mason Eagers 2021
Illustrations © Anna Platts 2021
Design © Lorna Gray 2021

First printed 2021
This edition 2024

The rights of Dinah Mason Eagers and Anna Platts to be identified as the author and illustrator respectively of this work has been asserted by them in accordance with the Copyright, Designs and Patents Act 1988.

All rights reserved. No part of this publication may be reproduced, stored in a retrieval system, or transmitted in any form or by any means, electronic, mechanical, photocopying, recording or otherwise, without the prior permission of the copyright owner.

Typeset in Houschka Rounded

All our books are printed on FSC® certified paper from managed woodlands and recycled material. Printed in the UK by ESP Colour, Swindon.

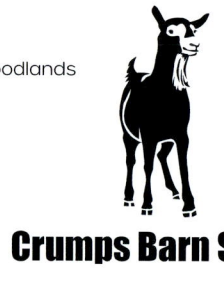

Crumps Barn Studio

ISBN 978-1-8382298-6-3

At the bottom of Dudley's Garden

story by *Dinah Mason Eagers*

illustrations by *Anna Platts*

Lily Katinka thought she was the most special and beautiful flower in Dudley's garden.

The other flowers admired her elegance very much.

Dudley himself thought that all the flowers in his garden were very special, including those at the bottom of the garden.

What was at the bottom of the garden?

At the bottom of the garden was a wildflower meadow, where the grass grew long and wildflowers spread freely.

It was the favourite part of the garden for the bees and butterflies. They loved the meadow flowers and spent many hours each day among them.

Now, Lily Katinka had pride of place in the flower bed next to the patio, where Dudley often sat out in the summer evenings with a slice of his favourite apple pie.

From there Lily Katinka could see everything in the garden. She could see Daffy Dahlia and Lulu Lupin smiling away in the sunshine.

She could see Sweet Penelope Pea climbing the willow canes, and Portia Peony looking fabulously flouncy in her special corner.

It troubled Lily Katinka when Dudley stopped mowing the end of the lawn and started letting the grass and weeds grow there.

She could not understand why part of the garden, which now looked so untidy, got so much attention from the bees, the butterflies and even from Dudley himself.

One day Lily Katinka decided she had to say something. "They are just ugly weeds down there!" she told the butterflies.

"They are just scruffy grasses down there!" she told the bees.

"Oh no Lily Katinka," they cried, "you are quite wrong! Those are the most important flowers in the garden! You should get to know them!"

This made Lily Katinka rather worried and just a little bit cross. She thought she was the most important flower in the garden. What was so special about those weeds? She had to find out.

The next time a buzzing bee was feeding on her pollen she asked the bee to tell her the names of the weeds.

"Well," said the bee, "they are: Humphrey Comfrey, Chloe Clover, Harebell Helene ...

"... and Pippa Poppy and Cornflower Blue.

"They are really nice and they are helping to save the planet!"

With that, the bee buzzed away to the next flower, Daffy Dahlia, but struggled to get to the pollen among Daffy's many overlapping petals.

So the bee gave up and went back to the wildflowers, which were very easy to feed from.

Soon the bee was back,
with lots of bee friends.

"We need to tell you something Lily!" they buzzed.

"It's about the wildflowers. We need them. They are full of pollen and without them there just wouldn't be enough food for us to eat."

"It is our job to travel from flower to flower, spreading pollen as we go. This is called pollination and it's what plants need to produce fruit and vegetables.

"But if there isn't enough pollen for us, we bees will die out – and poor Dudley wouldn't even be able to have apple pie any more. The apples wouldn't grow."

"Well, I had no idea," said Lily Katinka. She was now very worried about Dudley.

"I have certainly learned my lesson. Those wildflowers are very special and I should never have said they were ugly. You bees need them very much and so does Dudley – and all the humans.

"I am very glad such special flowers are in the same garden as me."

Now every time Dudley came and sat on the patio by her to eat his apple pie, Lily Katinka was very happy that he had let the wildflowers grow at the bottom of the garden. And so were the bees.

At the bottom of Dudley's garden, Humphrey Comfrey, Chloe Clover, Harebell Helene, Pippa Poppy, Cornflower Blue and all their wildflower friends were very glad that they were now welcomed into the garden by the other flowers.

They could see Lily Katinka smiling and waving in the wind at them from the patio and they smiled and waved back.

And Lily Katinka made a promise to herself that she would never again judge flowers by their petals.

The End

Did you know?

Bees collect nectar and pollen from flowers. Honey bees carry the nectar and pollen back to their hives where they turn nectar into honey, and pollen into an extraordinary food called bee bread. Bees eat a little honey and bread through the summer, but they also store it for winter so that they have plenty to eat during the cold months.

Bees have five eyes! If you look closely the next time a bee lands on a flower, you can see two big eyes on either side of their head, and three little dots on top too. These extra eyes help them to keep a lookout for danger while they're getting on with the important job of collecting pollen and nectar.

One in three mouthfuls of food we eat depends on a pollinator. You can help the bees and butterflies in your garden simply by letting white clover grow in your lawn. You could also plant a wildflower patch, or you could even mix pretty wildflowers with your favourite garden flowers — they'll look beautiful together!

Dinah